STAR WARS®

THE CLONE WARS™

AMBUSH

Adapted by Zachary Rau

Grosset & Dunlap · LucasBooks

GROSSET & DUNLAP

Published by the Penguin Group

Penguin Group (USA) Inc., 375 Hudson Street, New York, New York 10014, USA

Penguin Group (Canada), 90 Eglinton Avenue East, Suite 700,

Toronto, Ontario M4P 2Y3, Canada

(a division of Pearson Penguin Canada Inc.)

Penguin Books Ltd., 80 Strand, London WC2R 0RL, England

Penguin Group Ireland, 25 St. Stephen's Green, Dublin 2, Ireland

(a division of Penguin Books Ltd.)

Penguin Group (Australia), 250 Camberwell Road, Camberwell, Victoria 3124, Australia

(a division of Pearson Australia Group Pty. Ltd.)

Penguin Books India Pvt. Ltd., 11 Community Centre, Panchsheel Park,

New Delhi—110 017, India

Penguin Group (NZ), 67 Apollo Drive, Rosedale, North Shore 0632, New Zealand

(a division of Pearson New Zealand Ltd.)

Penguin Books (South Africa) (Pty.) Ltd., 24 Sturdee Avenue,

Rosebank, Johannesburg 2196, South Africa

Penguin Books Ltd., Registered Offices:

80 Strand, London WC2R 0RL, England

This book is published in partnership with LucasBooks, a division of Lucasfilm Ltd.

Library of Congress Control Number: 2008029141

ISBN 978-0-448-45039-1   10 9 8 7 6 5 4 3 2 1

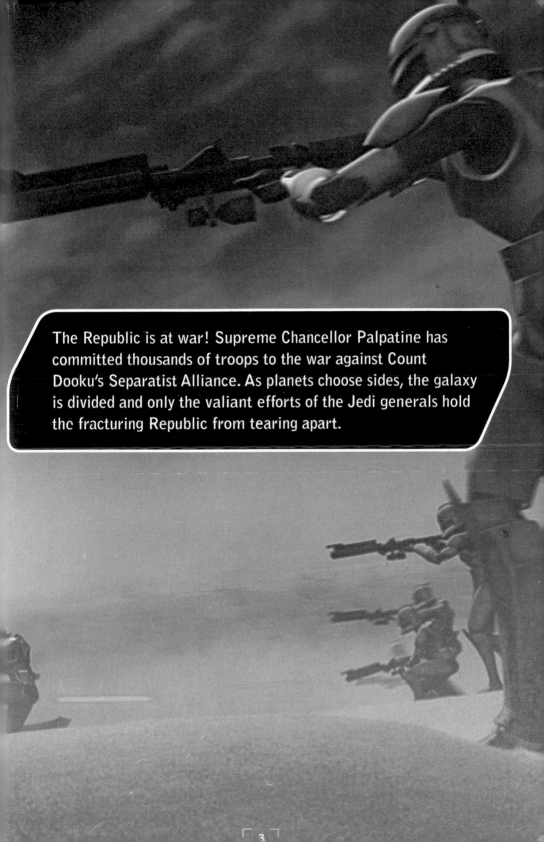

The Republic is at war! Supreme Chancellor Palpatine has committed thousands of troops to the war against Count Dooku's Separatist Alliance. As planets choose sides, the galaxy is divided and only the valiant efforts of the Jedi generals hold the fracturing Republic from tearing apart.

Peaceful worlds must choose sides or face the threat of invasion. Republic and Separatist armies vie for the allegiance of neutral planets.

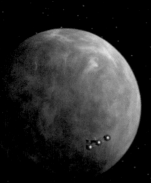

Desperate to build a Republic supply base in the system of Toydaria, Jedi Master Yoda travels to secret negotiations on a remote neutral moon.

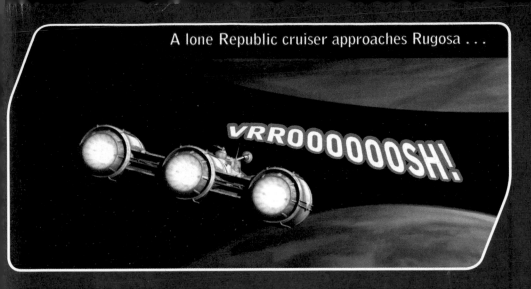

A lone Republic cruiser approaches Rugosa . . .

VRROOOOOOSH!

On the bridge, Clone Captain Zak hails the planet.

TOYDARIAN ROYAL DELEGATION, THIS IS THE REPUBLIC ENVOY. PLEASE RESPOND. TOYDARIAN DELEGATION, PLEASE RESPOND!

GENERAL YODA, THE TOYDARIAN'S BEACON IS ACTIVE ON THE MOON, BUT ALL OUR TRANSMISSIONS ARE BEING JAMMED.

HMMM . . .

On the surface of Rugosa, the Toydarians are having the same problem.

?!

WE'RE GETTING NO SIGNAL FROM THE REPUBLIC, YOUR HIGHNESS.

I DON'T SEE ANYTHING! IT IS NOT LIKE THE JEDI TO BE LATE.

At that moment, Count Dooku's assassin Asajj Ventress steps out of the shadows . . .

I AM ONLY A MESSENGER, MAJESTY. MY MASTER WISHES TO SPEAK WITH YOU.

Ventress produces a small holoprojector . . .

FWISH!

. . . and throws it to the ground.

KATUUNKO, GREAT KING OF TOYDARIA, FORGIVE MY INTRUSION.

An image of Count Dooku, the leader of the Separatist movement, appears in front of the Toydarian king.

I AM AWARE THAT MASTER YODA HOPES YOU WILL ALLOW THE JEDI TO BUILD A REPUBLIC BASE IN YOUR SYSTEM. IN EXCHANGE FOR PROTECTION, CORRECT?

YOUR SPIES SERVE YOU WELL, COUNT DOOKU.

I ASK, HOW CAN THE JEDI PROTECT YOU IF THEY CANNOT PROTECT THEMSELVES?

As Yoda's cruiser approaches the moon, a Banking Clan ship drops out of hyperspace and immediately opens fire on them.

Another Banking Clan frigate drops out of hyperspace directly behind the Republic vessel.

And just like that the Republic ship is caught in a cross fire.

ALL BATTERIES RETURN FIRE!

GET US OUT OF HERE! WE'RE LOSING OUR SHIELDS!

I MUST GET YOU TO SAFETY, GENERAL—

TOO LATE IT IS. SPRUNG IS THE TRAP!

RETREAT YOU MUST! ON THE MOON BELOW IS MY MISSION, THERE I WILL GO!

Yoda and three clone troopers climb into an escape pod and prepare to land on the planet.

The Republic frigate launches all the ship's escape pods . . .

. . . including one that contains the Republic envoy.

Back on Rugosa . . .

MASTER YODA'S POWERS HAVE BEEN GREATLY EXAGGERATED.

INDEED! WHEN YOU DECIDE TO JOIN US MY APPRENTICE WILL CONTACT ME.

THAT REMAINS TO BE SEEN, COUNT.

MY LORD, MASTER YODA'S WARSHIP HAS FLED THE SYSTEM.

WHAT FURTHER EVIDENCE DO YOU REQUIRE OF THE JEDI'S WEAKNESS?

As Count Dooku's holoprojection signs off, the Toydarians notice the space battle high above.

Suddenly, King Katuunko's holoprojector begins to sound, signaling an incoming message.

THIS IS KING KATUUNKO, SPEAK!

MASTER YODA WOULD LIKE TO SPEAK WITH YOU, SIR.

Katuunko clicks on the projector and an image of Clone Lieutenant Thire appears.

A PLEASURE IT IS TO HEAR YOUR VOICE, YOUR HIGHNESS. MASTER YODA OF THE JEDI COUNCIL, THIS IS.

MASTER YODA, I THOUGHT PERHAPS COUNT DOOKU HAD FRIGHTENED YOU OFF.

DELAYED I HAVE BEEN, BUT NOT TOO FAR AWAY AM I NOW. UNAWARE I WAS, COUNT DOOKU WAS INVITED TO OUR MEETING.

THE COUNT INVITED HIMSELF. HE ASSURES ME THAT IN THIS TIME OF WAR HIS DROIDS CAN OFFER MY WORLD GREATER SECURITY THAN YOU JEDI.

HMMMPH . . . A MATTER OF DEBATE THAT IS.

YOUR MAJESTY MIGHT PREFER MORE THAN WORDS.

IF YODA IS INDEED THE JEDI WARRIOR YOU BELIEVE HE IS, LET HIM PROVE IT. ALLOW ME TO SEND MY BEST TROOPS TO *CAPTURE* HIM.

WHAT DID YOU HAVE IN MIND?

IF HE ESCAPES, JOIN THE REPUBLIC, BUT SHOULD MY DROIDS DEFEAT YODA, CONSIDER AN ALLIANCE WITH THE SEPARATISTS.

I DID NOT REQUEST YODA'S PRESENCE HERE TO TEST HIM IN BATTLE.

ACCEPT THE CHALLENGE I DO, YOUR HIGHNESS. ARRIVE BY NIGHTFALL, I WILL.

MASTER YODA MUST BE GIVEN A FAIR FIGHT.

MY DEAR KING KATUUNKO, I WOULD HAVE IT NO OTHER WAY.

A familiar sound distracts the Republic envoy.

Elsewhere . . .

I AM DEPLOYING MY FORCES, MASTER.

YODA HAS MADE A GRAVE MISTAKE STRAYING THIS FAR FROM CORUSCANT.

I WILL SEE THE JEDI GETS HIS *FAIR FIGHT.*

HE'LL BE THE SMALL SHRIVELED GREEN ONE WITH THE LIGHTSABER!

SMALL, HUH? DON'T WORRY, SUPREME LEADER, WE'LL TAKE CARE OF HIM.

Later, the droid army searches for Yoda and the three clones.

I THINK I SEE THEM. THEY'RE HIDING DEEP IN THE TREES!

FIRE ON SECTOR ELEVEN!

The droid tanks fire on the clones with no success.

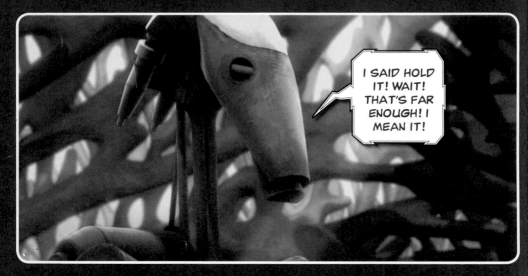

THOSE TANKS ARE TOO BIG TO FOLLOW!

SEE? SIZE IS NOT EVERYTHING. SMALLER IN NUMBER WE ARE, BUT LARGER IN MIND.

DO YOU HAVE ANY IDEA WHAT THE GENERAL IS TALKING ABOUT?

SIR, THERE ARE TWO PATROLS COMING IN ON FOOT!

NOW IS THE TIME TO FACE THE ENEMY, LIEUTENANT! AMBUSH THEM WE WILL.

WE'LL FLANK THEM FROM THE SOUTH!

RIGHT, LET'S MOVE!

CLANG! CLANG! CLANG! CLANG!

As the droid army advances . . .

CLANG! CLANG! CLANG! CLANG!

. . . the clones hide and wait to spring their trap.

CLANG! CLANG! CLANG! CLANG!

BZZZZKT!

SPLIT UP BY SQUAD AND SPREAD OUT.

BLAM!

As one clone distracts the droids, the other two open fire behind the droids . . .

. . . destroying them all.

Suddenly, a squad of battle droids appears.

HE'S AROUND HERE SOMEWHERE!

Elsewhere, Yoda is perched in a coral tree planning his next move!

HEH!

HEY! GET OFF ME!

Yoda jumps onto the back of a droid.

DON'T MOVE!

BLAM!

The droids begin shooting wildly at Yoda, who jumps from droid to droid, tricking them into destroying one another with friendly fire . . .

. . . until only two remain.

The Master Jedi patiently waits while the droids try to figure out what to do.

The overexcited droids shoot at Yoda, who merely ducks . . .

. . . as the droids destroy themselves.

On the other side of the moon . . .

THE JEDI DESTROYED OUR ADVANCE TROOPS.

MASTER YODA IS LIVING UP TO MY EXPECTATIONS.

COMMANDER, HAVE YOU PINPOINTED THE JEDI'S LOCATION?

I HOPE THE GENERAL REACHES THE RENDEZVOUS POINT.

HUFF! HUFF!

Back in the coral forest, the clones run from a squad of super battle droids.

WE'RE SURE BUYING HIM TIME!

AFFIRMATIVE. THE CLONES GAVE AWAY THEIR POSITION. OUR HEAVY TROOPS ARE MOVING TO ENGAGE THEM NOW.

KABOOM!

ARRRGH!

As they retreat, Lieutenant Thire is hit by a laser blast.

DIE, REPUBLIC DOGS!!

LIEUTENANT, CAN YOU WALK?

YEAH, I'M OKAY.

Yoda jumps out of the forest . . .

. . . to buy the clones some time.

WHAT ARE WE GOING TO DO, SIR?

Clone trooper Jjeck pulls the wounded lieutenant out of the way, but they all end up pinned down behind a rock unable to escape.

WHAT'S THE GENERAL DOING?!

Much to the surprise of his clone troopers, Yoda turns off his lightsaber and begins to meditate.

KEEP BLASTING!

BLAM!

BLAM!

BLAM!

Without the guidance of the Jedi, the clones struggle to keep the droid army at bay.

Amid the frenzy of enemy fire, Yoda peacefully concentrates on the Force . . .

HEY! WHAT'S GOING ON?!

. . . lifting a super battle droid into the air.

GET OUT OF THE WAY! ALL OF YOU!

KZZZAK!

BOOM!

The droid suddenly turns on the rest of its squad . . .

...destroying them all.

YOU FOUND US JUST IN TIME, SIR.

LEFT BEHIND, NO ONE WILL BE.

All of a sudden, the clones hear a chilling and familiar sound.

KLANK! KLANK! KLANK! KLANK!
KLANK! KLANK! KLANK! KLANK!

ROLLIES INBOUND!

Three destroyer droids roll into view.

Yoda again jumps into the fray to buy the clones time.

Realizing that they are outgunned, Yoda must make a decision.

RETREAT! COVER YOU, I WILL!

THE REPUBLIC TROOPS ARE INJURED. THE JEDI IS IN FULL RETREAT, SUPREME LEADER!

GOOD! PURSUE THEM WITHOUT DELAY.

King Katuunko pulls out his holoprojector to contact the Jedi.

THE CONTEST IS NOT OVER YET.

Filled with anger, Ventress grabs the projector . . .

. . . and crushes it!

Just outside the coral forest . . .

. . . Yoda finds a cave to rest in.

ARE YOU SURE WE SHOULD GO IN THERE, GENERAL? THERE'S NO WAY OUT!

NOW REST, WE MUST!

Inside the cave . . .

WE'RE LOW ON AMMO, SIR. ONLY TWO GRENADES AND ONE ROCKET FOR THE LAUNCHER.

CLICK!

AGAINST A BATTALION?! FORGET IT! WE'VE LOST!

SO CERTAIN OF DEFEAT ARE YOU, HMMM?

WITH RESPECT, GENERAL, MAYBE YOU SHOULD GO ON. LET US SLOW 'EM DOWN!

For the first time since arriving on Rugosa, the clones feel hopeful.

Not even the sound of an approaching tank division can dampen their spirits.

HAVE YOU THREE I DO! OUTNUMBERED THEY ARE.

KNOW THE TIME TO HELP ME, YOU WILL!

WHOOSH!

HMMM...

IT'S THE JEDI! BLOCK HIS ESCAPE!

SUPREME LEADER, WE'VE FOUND THE JEDI!

EXCELLENT! WHERE IS HE?

HE'S JUST SITTING HERE IN FRONT OF OUR TANKS.

SHOOT HIM! SHOOT HIM NOW!

QUICKLY, READY! AIM! FIRE! **FIRE!**

KA-BOOM!

Yoda cuts a whole in the bottom of the tank and jumps into it.

MAKE A RUN FOR IT!

OH NO!

All is quiet until . . .

IT DOESN'T LOOK LIKE THE GENERAL NEEDS HELP TO ME!

THAT'S A LOT OF SMOKE FOR A SURRENDER!

REPORT!

I THINK PERHAPS ALL THESE STORIES ABOUT THE JEDI ARE TRUE.

THE FIGHT ISN'T OVER YET, MAJESTY.

Ventress hits the communicator on her wrist and signals a fresh squad of droids.

THE GENERAL IS CUTTING 'EM UP!

WE GOT TROUBLE!

RUMBLE! RUMBLE!

THE CLANKERS SENT IN REINFORCEMENTS!

THE GENERAL'S TOO BUSY WITH THAT TANK!

HE WON'T SEE THEM COMING!

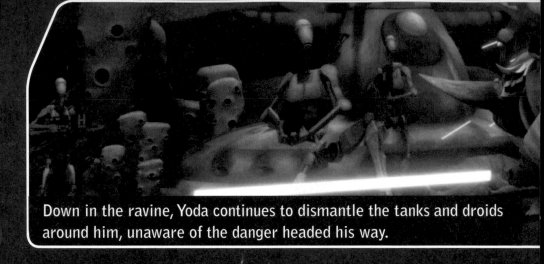

Down in the ravine, Yoda continues to dismantle the tanks and droids around him, unaware of the danger headed his way.

KSSSSSHT!

BOOM!

VSSSSKT!

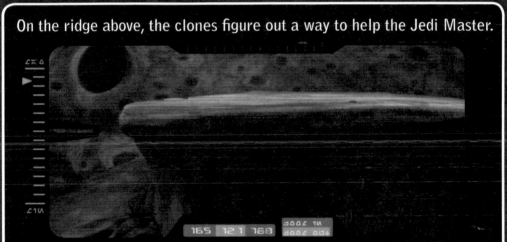

On the ridge above, the clones figure out a way to help the Jedi Master.

765 127 788

I THINK I KNOW HOW TO DEAL WITH THEM.

At that moment, Yoda notices droidekas approaching and prepares himself for a fight.

FWOOSH!

Lieutenant Thire launches a single rocket . . .

. . . aimed at an overhanging rock directly above the destroyer droids.

The rocket hits the target and . . .

. . . rains down boulder-sized rocks onto the destroyer droids . . .

. . . smashing them all.

With the battle over, Yoda meditates to conserve his energy as he waits for the clones to join him.

A birdlike neebray senses the peace and calm in Yoda . . .

. . . and lands on his finger, unafraid.

Yoda and the neebray sit together . . .

HMMMM . . . !

FWIP! FWIP! FWIP!

LEARNED SOMETHING TODAY HAVE YOU, LIEUTENANT?

. . . until the presence of the clones startles the creature and it flies off.

I THINK WE ALL DID, GENERAL.

COME. BEHIND SCHEDULE ARE WE. NOT POLITE TO BE LATE!

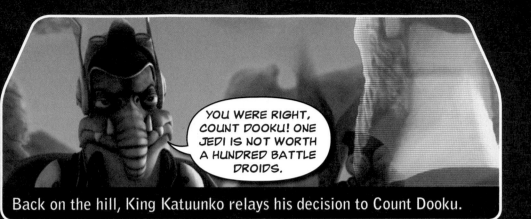

YOU WERE RIGHT, COUNT DOOKU! ONE JEDI IS NOT WORTH A HUNDRED BATTLE DROIDS.

Back on the hill, King Katuunko relays his decision to Count Dooku.

MORE LIKE A THOUSAND!

I'M SORRY, BUT I WILL BE JOINING THE REPUBLIC.

I URGE YOU TO RECONSIDER, WISE KING! I PROMISE YOU WON'T REGRET IT.

Ventress ignites her lightsabers and prepares to follow her orders.

Immediately, Toydarian guards step in front of their king, determined to protect him.

Ventress easily dispatches the guards with a single Force-push.

OOOF!

UNH!

CRASH!

As Ventress prepares to strike the final blow . . .

. . . Yoda uses his mastery of the Force to freeze her.

No matter how hard Ventress struggles, she is unable to move.

Yoda turns toward Ventress and, with a flick of the wrist, sends her sliding backward.

STRONG YOU ARE WITH THE DARK SIDE, YOUNG ONE, BUT NOT THAT STRONG.

STILL MUCH TO LEARN YOU HAVE.

To prove his point, Yoda waves his hand . . .

. . . and Force-pulls both of Ventress's lightsabers from her hands.

SURRENDER, YOU SHOULD.

Realizing she is overmatched, Ventress races to her ship . . .

. . . and makes a quick getaway.

IN THE END, COWARDS ARE THOSE WHO FOLLOW THE DARK SIDE.

IT'S A PITY I WASN'T THERE IN PERSON, MY OLD MASTER.

A PITY INDEED, MY FALLEN APPRENTICE.

YOUR MAJESTY, FAIL YOU, WE WILL NOT!

The Republic cruiser reenters the system as Republic forces swarm the planet to provide protection from any remaining Separatist droids.

Yoda and King Katuunko board a gunship to make plans for the Republic's base and to seal their agreement.

The end.

Bonus Adventure!
Cloak of Darkness

Viceroy Gunray captured! Senator Padmé Amidala has scored a victory against the Separatist Alliance on the remote world of Rodia by securing the arrest of diabolical confederate leader Nute Gunray.

The Jedi Council has dispatched Master Luminara Unduli and Padawan Ahsoka Tano to escort the Viceroy to Coruscant under heavy guard. Once there, he will face trial for his many war crimes.

CAPTAIN, HAVE YOU MADE CONTACT WITH THE CRUISER?

YES, GENERAL. WE'LL PATCH YOU THROUGH NOW.

JEDI CRUISER *TRANQUILITY*, THIS IS GENERAL LUMINARA UNDULI REQUESTING PERMISSION TO LAND.

YOU ARE CLEARED, GENERAL. WE AWAIT YOUR PRISONER'S ARRIVAL.

IT'S GUNRAY'S ARMY WE HAVE TO WORRY ABOUT. WE MUST BE CAUTIOUS!

HOW DOES A MONEY-GRUBBING WORM LIKE GUNRAY RATE ALL THIS SECURITY?

As the Jedi seal the Viceroy into a holding cell, the cruiser is rocked by laser blasts.

BOOM! BOOM! BOOM!

DROID FIGHTERS INCOMING! THEY'VE BROUGHT BOARDING SHIPS!

SUPER BATTLE DROIDS HAVE BREACHED OUR HULL!

Before anyone knows what has happened, the entire ship is plunged into chaos.

KZZZ! KZZZ!

THEY'RE HEADED FOR THE DETENTION LEVEL!

WE NEED REINFORCEMENTS!

COMMANDER, I'LL NEED YOUR ASSISTANCE.

AHSOKA, YOU WILL STAY HERE WITH CAPTAIN ARGYUS. GUARD THE VICEROY!

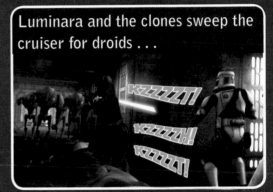

Luminara and the clones sweep the cruiser for droids . . .

KZZZZT!

KZZZZH!

KZZZZT!

. . . clearing out the ship level by level.

THAT LOOKS LIKE THE LAST OF THEM, GENERAL.

YES, COMMANDER, BUT I SENSE OUR TROUBLES ARE NOT OVER.

SOUNDS LIKE YOUR RESCUE DIDN'T WORK!

Back at the Viceroy's holding cell . . .

I—I AM READY TO DISCUSS A BARGAIN AGAIN.

Argyus, the captain of the Jedi cruiser, approaches the Padawan.

PADAWAN TANO, MAY I HAVE A WORD WITH YOU?

CERTAINLY, CAPTAIN.

I'VE GOT THE ALL CLEAR. THE ENEMY HAS BEEN REPELLED.

AND THEIR ATTEMPT TO FREE GUNRAY HAS . . .

Ahsoka is interrupted by the sound of lightsabers cutting through reinforced steel.

Asajj Ventress jumps out of the hole and takes out the Senate guards and Captain Argyus.

IF IT ISN'T SKYWALKER'S FILTHY, OBNOXIOUS LITTLE PET.

STAND DOWN AND I'LL GIVE YOU A COOKIE.

HOW NICE OF YOU! TELL YOU WHAT . . . I'LL GIVE YOU A MERCIFUL DEATH.

The dark assassin uses her power to push past the apprentice . . .

. . . and free Gunray.

HALT, ASSASSIN!

Luminara rushes in to help Ahsoka.

SURRENDER!

WHOOSH!

Using the Force . . .

. . . Ventress makes a quick escape down a turbolift shaft.

OUR ATTACKER HAS COME FOR GUNRAY. STAY HERE AND GUARD HIM. I'LL CONFRONT HER MYSELF.

I CAN'T LET HER FACE THAT LOWLIFE ALONE. WOULDN'T WE HAVE A BETTER CHANCE OF STOPPING HER IF I HELPED?

SOMETIMES BEING A GOOD SOLDIER MEANS DOING WHAT YOU THINK IS RIGHT. THAT IS WHY WE'RE SUPERIOR TO DROIDS.

With that, Ahsoka disobeys her orders and jumps down the turbolift shaft.

Suddenly, Captain Argyus turns on the two Senate guards and shoots them down.

NO, PLEASE DON'T!

OH, DO SHUT UP! COUNT DOOKU IS PAYING ME A FORTUNE TO DELIVER YOUR SLIMY CARCASS.

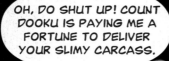

Using the Viceroy as a living shield, Captain Argyus heads toward the Republic frigate housed in the belly of the *Tranquility*.

Onboard the frigate, Argyus starts the launch sequence . . .

THE OUTER SHIELDS ARE STILL DOWN! THE SHIP IS STILL IN TURMOIL! WE'RE HOME FREE!

AS SUCCESSFUL A RESCUE AS ONE COULD HOPE FOR, VICEROY. I'LL BE A LEGEND FOR THIS.

YOU SEE, ASSASSIN, OUR PLAN WENT OFF WITHOUT A HITCH.

The door to the bridge opens and Ventress strides in, having evaded both Jedi.

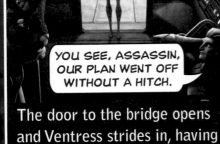

AND I WILL, OF COURSE, MAKE SURE YOUR CONTRIBUTIONS ARE NOTED IN MY REPORT TO COUNT DOOKU.

I'LL TELL HIM MYSELF!

VZZZZZZH!

True to her nature, Ventress betrays Argyus and pierces his heart with a lightsaber.

I ALWAYS HAD A GOOD FEELING ABOUT YOU, ASSASSIN!

A COWARD VICEROY GUNRAY IS, BUT POWERFUL ALLIES HE HAS! SWIFTLY WE MUST MOVE, IF WE ARE TO RECAPTURE HIM.

AHSOKA, I'LL MEET YOU AT THE RENDEZVOUS POINT.

YES, MASTER.

MASTER LUMINARA, I GUESS THIS IS GOOD-BYE FOR NOW.

THANK YOU, MASTER!

FAREWELL.

The end.